CONTENTS

Words that look like *this* can be accessed in the <<GLOSSARY>> on page 31

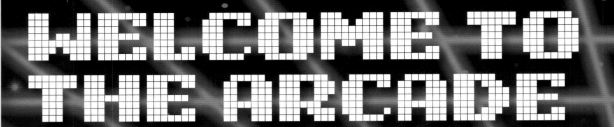

WELCOME TO THE ARCADE

Today's the day of the big esports tournament. I've been working on my thumb muscles for ages. Are you ready? Then let's go!

Ever since the very first video game – and before that, ever since the first caveman threw the first rock a little farther than the caveman next to him – people have liked to compete with one another. Do you love the thrill of the chase, or is crossing the finish line first all that matters? If it takes a brave family member to suggest a board game after dinner in your house, then you've come to the right place: today's all about competitive games. This gaming guide will help you to build your skills, and rise from the crowd to the top of the podium in the world of competitive games. So, what are you waiting for – GET YOUR GAME ON!

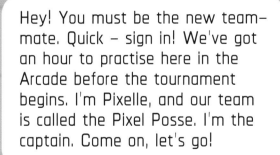

Hey! You must be the new team-mate. Quick – sign in! We've got an hour to practise here in the Arcade before the tournament begins. I'm Pixelle, and our team is called the Pixel Posse. I'm the captain. Come on, let's go!

Let's start with the basics. A video game is an **electronic** game that needs a player (that's you) to use a device (that's the thing you play on) to make stuff happen on a screen. Usually, that screen is a television or a computer monitor, but you can play games on mobile phones, hand-held gaming devices or tablets too. To play on your television you will need a console – this is a special type of computer just for playing video games. If you play on a computer screen you will probably use a PC. This stands for personal computer and is a type of computer designed to be used at home by regular people for lots of things – like doing homework or using the internet – and playing games, of course! There are lots of types of video games. From **pixel**-perfect platformers and puzzlers to amazing action-adventure games that will see you virtually risking virtual life and limb, there is something in video games for everyone.

Ok, team. I want fingers on **shoulder buttons**, thumbs at the ready, and reflexes all stretched. In this training session I'm going to push you hard so that, in the tournament, we can be the winners! Let's go!

<<Player One... Ready...?>>

ARCADE

DATA FILE: ONLINE AND MULTIPLAYER GAMES

Arcade – we're ready to start. Load data.

<<LOADING... DATA LEVEL ONE: WHAT IS A MULTIPLAYER GAME>>

While lots of games can be enjoyed alone at home or on a handheld console, other games let us play against other people, either via local area networks *(LAN)* or the internet. People have been playing games together over the phone lines since we were able to send the data, but since the internet became universally popular in the 1990s, games and player interaction has become more and more complicated. As technology has improved, so has our ability to play games against other people online, and now, thanks to *4G*, players can even challenge each other from their mobile phones while they sit on the bus on the way to school. Whether you like playing word and puzzle games, strategy titles, shooters, or massively multiplayer online role-playing games (or MMORPGs for short), it's never been easier to play with people around the world. Lots of games can be played with more than one player. Some are even played professionally, especially sports games, shooters and *MOBAs*.

 64:27 ENG 2 - 0 DEN

PLAYER INDICATOR

MATCH INFORMATION

OPPONENT

TEAMMATE

PLAYER INFORMATION

9 PIXELLE

PITCH MAP

ESPORTS

The very best players compete for the biggest prizes in gaming. The most popular games attract huge audiences and the pros can do some incredible things with a controller or mouse.

SPORTS GAMES

Sports games are **simulations** often including real kits, players, and stadiums. FIFA is probably the most famous, but most popular sports are turned into video games.

SHOOTERS

Games like Overwatch and Fortnite allow players to go into online battles armed to the teeth with crazy weapons and spectacular superpowers.

MMORPGS

Role-playing games started on the table, but soon, players realised they could go on adventures together online. Games like World of Warcraft offer whole worlds to explore.

FREE-TO-PLAY

Titles like World of Tanks are free to download, although players can also buy **unique** units, boosters to help them in-game and decorative items to make them look unique.

PERSISTENT WORLDS

Some games never sleep. With huge armies fighting in Planetside 2 and strategy battles in mobile games like Clash of Clans, the frontlines are always moving.

<<KILLER BYTES>>
IT IS ESTIMATED THAT POPULAR BATTLE ROYALE
GAME FORTNITE MADE 1.5 MILLION DOLLARS
IN ITS FIRST THREE DAYS ONLINE.

7

BLIZZCON

A gaming convention is a huge event in any gamer's social calendar. Conventions are large gatherings of people who all share an interest – be that a specific game, a brand such as Nintendo, or just video games in general. They all meet up over 2–3 days at a special event, and play games, dress up as their favourite characters, buy merchandise, and sometimes meet the stars of their favourite games in person!

WORLD OF WARCRAFT

STARCRAFT II

DIABLO

HEARTHSTONE

For MMO fans, BlizzCon has to be the most important of them all. Blizzard, who make games such as World of Warcraft, Starcraft and Overwatch, hold the convention every year in Anaheim, California. Fans of Blizzard games are treated to two days of game news, previews of new games, costume contests and hands–on play on games such as Diablo, Heroes of the Storm and Hearthstone. The convention (or 'con') closes with a concert, and fans are treated to a goodie bag with treats, games and more.

COSPLAY

What do you get when you add costumes to play: cosplay! Cosplay is a performance art where people dress up as characters from their favourite games, movies, books or TV shows. Often, people spend months making their costumes, paying attention to every tiny detail. Cosplayers use skills like mask–making, sculpting, makeup, wig–making and sewing to create their amazing costumes.

In cosplay, anyone can be anything. Cosplayers don't have to stick to their own gender, race or age, and can even mix up characters from different worlds or themes. When in costume, many cosplayers behave like the character too, speaking and moving as they do. At BlizzCon, there is even a competition that cosplayers can enter – and contests for artwork, movies and music based on the games.

TECH TALK

If you're going to get ahead in the competitive world of online gaming, you need to know what you're talking about. This data file will give you what you need to know to get started. Arcade; tell us what we need to know.

<<LOADING... DATA LEVEL THREE: WHAT YOU NEED TO KNOW>>

TAKE AIM

A lot of online games involve having a good aim: whether you're firing paint in Splatoon, shells in World of Tanks, or magic spells in World of Warcraft, a big part of the action is going to involve besting an opponent. You'll need to be calm and focused to emerge victorious, but also well rested. Take regular breaks when playing and you'll stay sharp.

LEARN THE LINGO

The communities that build up around online games often start to create their own languages and phrases. For example, GG stands for "good game", something that players say to each other if they've enjoyed the match. Learn the language and talk the talk, but remember to be respectful to your fellow players.

KNOW YOUR MODE

Multiplayer games come in all shapes and sizes, but within each game there are often different ways to play. These are called 'modes' and each one comes with different rules and settings. It's always super important to know what is going on in each mode and how the rules differ.

PLAY THE OBJECTIVE

This might sound like common sense, but you must always remember to play the objective. Far too often people get distracted or forget what they're doing, and in a close match it can make all the difference. Don't be dragged out of position and don't chase after personal glory – work as a team and work the objective.

DOMINATE THE MAP

In a lot of multiplayer games, the action takes place on different maps, and these maps are usually quite varied in terms of how they look. More importantly, each map has features that are advantageous to the team that occupies it, whether that be a high point that lets you see more of the area around, or a good hiding spot.

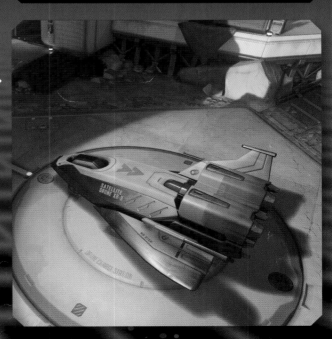

FACT FILE:

WORLD of WARCRAFT
BATTLE for AZEROTH

Blizzard's World of Warcraft – or WoW as it's often called – is one of the most famous games in the world, and at the peak of its powers it had millions of players logging in every day and going on fantastical adventures together with their friends. WoW is an MMORPG, which stands for massively multiplayer online role-playing game. That's a bit of a mouthful, but it basically means that it's a role-playing game that people play online together in groups.

Role-playing games usually let people create their own characters, often making them up from scratch. In WoW, players can be humans, orcs, elves, Pandarens and more. There's a huge range of options players can use to customise their character, something which lets people add interesting features to their made–up heroes to make them look unique and special. Once you get playing, the things you do earn points, which you can spend on *gearing up*.

Then comes the MMO part. With your special one-of-a-kind character you head off in search of adventure, teaming up with other players to explore dungeons and hunt for loot, or battle against challenging enemy bosses. One of the best things about WoW is it can also allow people to hang out – a big part of the experience is just hanging out with your friends.

Warcraft didn't start off as an MMORPG. Before Blizzard made this third-person role-playing game, it was a strategy series where players built settlements and controlled small armies. Since the success of WoW there's even been a big budget Hollywood movie and the fantasy world remains popular to this day.

GET YOUR GAME ON

Remember, guys, there is no "i" in "team – every player needs to make sure they practise, practise, practise, so their skills are sharp and they are always ready to compete. Let's look at some of the things we'll need to remember.

<<LOADING... DATA LEVEL FOUR: THINGS YOU'LL NEED TO KEEP IN MIND>>

BUILD YOURSELF

Some games offer a level playing field – every player goes into battle with the same gear and it's all about skill. Other games, however, allow you to build your character or team up over time. Spend time making sure you've upgraded your *loadout*/line–up so you're at full strength when you go up against human opponents.

PRACTISE AI

Before you take on other players, why not test yourself against the computer? Some online games come with tutorials which show you the ropes, while others have a short single–player *campaign* which might take four or five hours to complete but gives you a small taste of everything the game has to offer.

TAKE IT SLOW

Slow and steady is always advisable, especially when you're new to a game. Rushing into the action can often result in an untimely end, so it's always a good idea to put the brakes on before you *engage* the enemy and assess the situation. If you're outnumbered and outgunned, it might be better to avoid a particular fight.

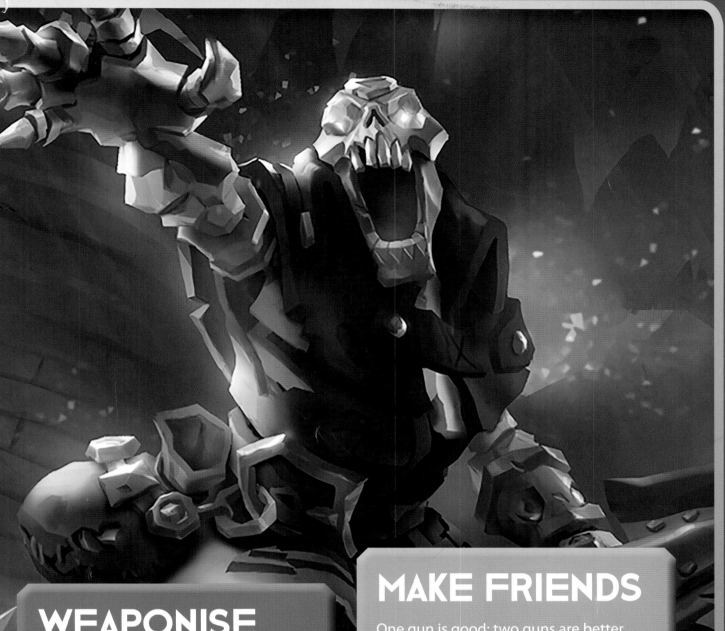

WEAPONISE

Every weapon (or player, if you're playing a sports game) has a *speciality*, and using them effectively and at the right time is the key to success. There's no point firing a sniper rifle up close, and using your goalkeeper up front means you won't score many goals.

MAKE FRIENDS

One gun is good; two guns are better. If you've got a friend by your side, your chances double, and if you and your opponent are evenly matched, your companion will make all the difference. Always pay attention to what your friends are doing, talk over a microphone if you've got one, and stick together whenever you've got the chance.

TIME YOUR MOVE

Whether you're waiting for a certain weapon to spawn on the map, or for a character's special ability to come online, part of successful play is timing your attack and making sure you're at your strongest when your enemy is at their weakest.

FACT FILE: EA SPORTS

EA Sports has developed a reputation over the years for making some of the very best sports games. The studio aims to create realistic experiences – called simulations – of different sports including football, ice hockey, and basketball. These games include a number of different ways to play, either alone, with people at home, or online against your friends. Let's take a look at the different ways you can play sports games.

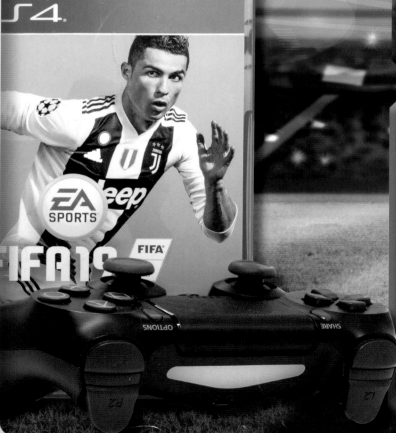

FIFA is a great example, and it's probably the most popular sports game in the world. With so many fans, it offers a whole range of ways to play. You can't always keep everyone happy, but EA certainly tries. For example, if you want to live the life of a real player you can take control of a young player and follow his career, taking part in games and controlling the action as you try to score important goals for the team. If you prefer a bit more control, you can become the manager of an entire team, making every decision from which players to sign to how much they should get paid. When you're not managing you also play the games, controlling the whole team in every match throughout a whole season.

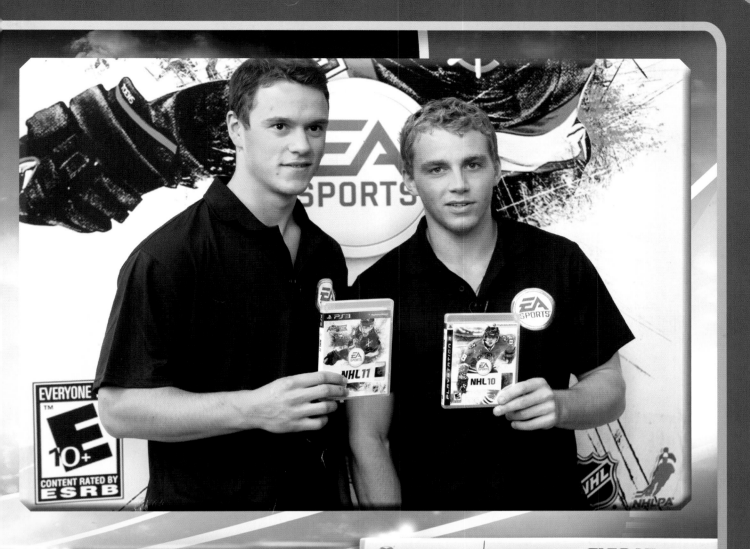

EVERYONE

E

10+

CONTENT RATED BY
ESRB

XBOX 360	FIFA 15
XBOX 360	FIFA 14
XBOX 360	FIFA 13
XBOX 360	FIFA 12
XBOX 360	FIFA 11
XBOX 360	FIFA 10
XBOX 360	FIFA 09
XBOX 360	FIFA 08
XBOX 360	FIFA 07
XBOX	FIFA 06
XBOX	FIFA Football 200
XBOX	FIFA Football 200
XBOX	FIFA FOOTBALL 2003

Of course, you can play against other people, either at home with your friends and family, or online against others. Players can control a team each, or lots of players can join in together and take on the role of just one player on a team, working together just as you would in a real football match. There are other competitive modes, like FIFA Ultimate Team – or FUT as lots of people call it – where you open packs that contain random players that you use to build a team, kind of like a sticker book.

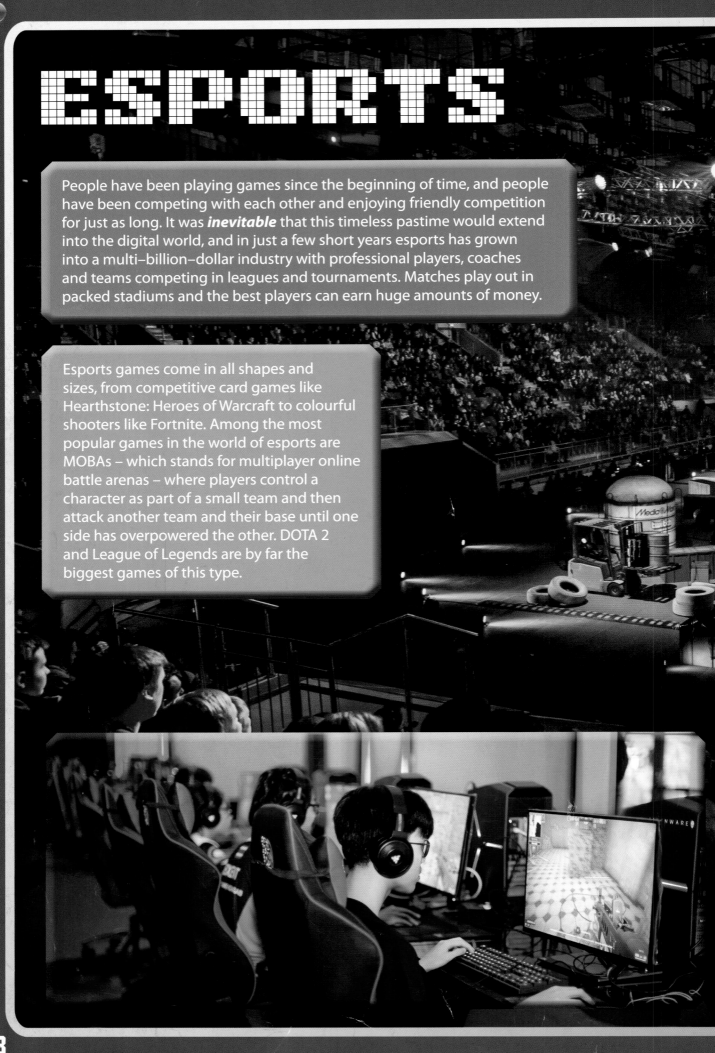

ESPORTS

People have been playing games since the beginning of time, and people have been competing with each other and enjoying friendly competition for just as long. It was *inevitable* that this timeless pastime would extend into the digital world, and in just a few short years esports has grown into a multi–billion–dollar industry with professional players, coaches and teams competing in leagues and tournaments. Matches play out in packed stadiums and the best players can earn huge amounts of money.

Esports games come in all shapes and sizes, from competitive card games like Hearthstone: Heroes of Warcraft to colourful shooters like Fortnite. Among the most popular games in the world of esports are MOBAs – which stands for multiplayer online battle arenas – where players control a character as part of a small team and then attack another team and their base until one side has overpowered the other. DOTA 2 and League of Legends are by far the biggest games of this type.

Cartoon–style competitive shooters like Overwatch and Splatoon 2 also attract plenty of interest and exist alongside military titles such as Call of Duty and Counter–Strike. Another shooter that has attracted a huge following is Fortnite, which started out as a base–building *co-op* game, but soon shot to superstardom thanks to its colourful and light–hearted approach to the battle royale formula that has every player fending for themselves. It doesn't hurt that it's free–to–play so that anyone who owns a console can get involved.

Esports is big business and the competitions building around the most popular games are drawing in huge crowds. Media outlets cover these competitions alongside regular sports, sponsors pay players and teams, and the best players are becoming celebrities in their own right with adoring fans and big prizes up for grabs.

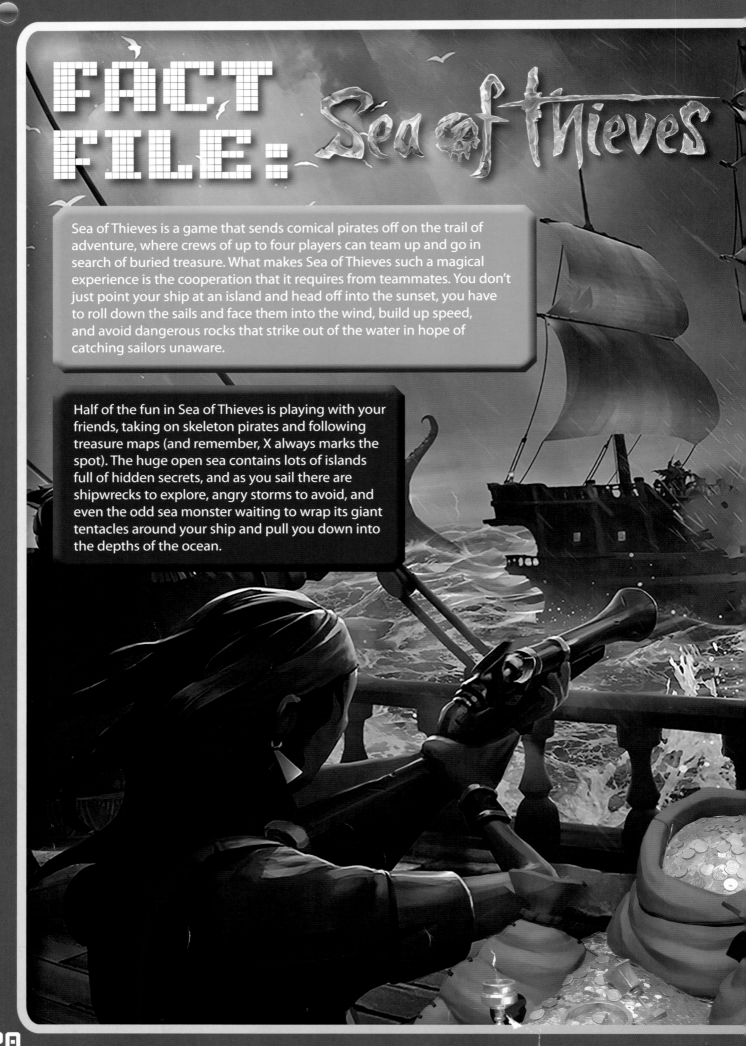

FACT FILE: Sea of Thieves

Sea of Thieves is a game that sends comical pirates off on the trail of adventure, where crews of up to four players can team up and go in search of buried treasure. What makes Sea of Thieves such a magical experience is the cooperation that it requires from teammates. You don't just point your ship at an island and head off into the sunset, you have to roll down the sails and face them into the wind, build up speed, and avoid dangerous rocks that strike out of the water in hope of catching sailors unaware.

Half of the fun in Sea of Thieves is playing with your friends, taking on skeleton pirates and following treasure maps (and remember, X always marks the spot). The huge open sea contains lots of islands full of hidden secrets, and as you sail there are shipwrecks to explore, angry storms to avoid, and even the odd sea monster waiting to wrap its giant tentacles around your ship and pull you down into the depths of the ocean.

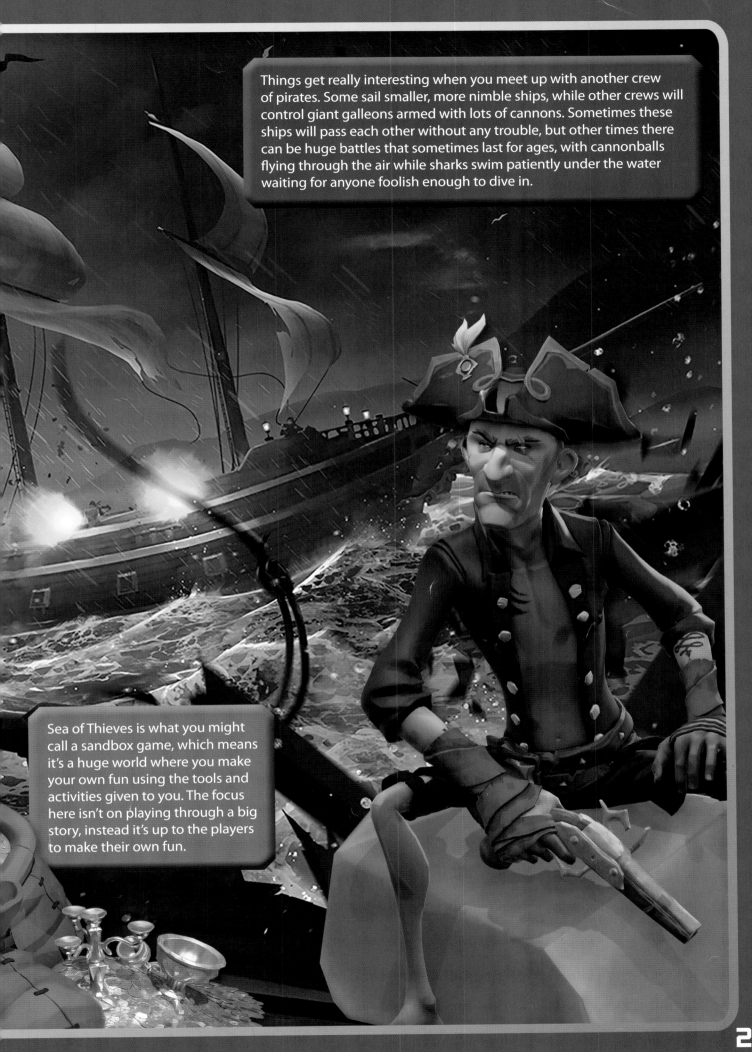

Things get really interesting when you meet up with another crew of pirates. Some sail smaller, more nimble ships, while other crews will control giant galleons armed with lots of cannons. Sometimes these ships will pass each other without any trouble, but other times there can be huge battles that sometimes last for ages, with cannonballs flying through the air while sharks swim patiently under the water waiting for anyone foolish enough to dive in.

Sea of Thieves is what you might call a sandbox game, which means it's a huge world where you make your own fun using the tools and activities given to you. The focus here isn't on playing through a big story, instead it's up to the players to make their own fun.

CONSOLE PROFILE

Microsoft has released three different Xbox consoles over the years, but could the latest spell the end of the old console generation cycle?

2000: XBOX

Data: The first Xbox console launched in 2000. Before that, Microsoft was best known for making operating systems and software. The console launched in the US first, and followed in Europe the following year. It was Microsoft's first move into the console space and the first time we saw the company's flagship title, Halo.

2004: XBOX LIVE

Data: Microsoft launched Xbox Live in early 2004. This online service brought players together for friendly online competition, but it was the launch of Halo 2 that really put Live on the map. For many console players it marked the first time they were able to play against other people from the comfort of their sofa.

2017: XBOX ONE X

Data: The Xbox brand looked to be in trouble, but after some soul-searching the company came back strong with the most powerful console the world has ever seen, the Xbox One X. The company also outlined its intentions to do away with the old console cycle, making many original Xbox and 360 titles compatible with the Xbox One, and suggesting a future where players will be able to take their libraries of games to all future consoles. They even opened up the platform to the PC space, with former exclusives now launching on Windows 10 PCs.

2005: XBOX 360

Data: The Xbox 360 put Microsoft ahead in the console wars, thanks in part to the move online, but also because of the exclusive games that appeared on the console. Halo returned, Gears of War and Forza both got started, and for a time, Microsoft's console was the console to own.

360 CONTROLLER

Data: Microsoft didn't get the controller for the first Xbox quite right, but the one that came with the Xbox 360 was best–in–class. The fact that it was not only an excellent controller but also PC compatible also helped it become the standard for PC gamers too.

2013: XBOX ONE

Data: When Microsoft announced the Xbox One the world wasn't quite ready for a lot of the ideas the company was suggesting and several features had to be scrapped before the console launched in late 2013.

2010: KINECT

Data: Kinect was a camera system that started on the 360 and ended on the Xbox One. It effectively turned the player's body into the controller, although it wasn't always smooth sailing and some games didn't quite deliver the experience the developers clearly wanted. The Kinect returned, bundled in with every Xbox One at launch, but the tech didn't catch on and in the end Microsoft had to ditch it.

FACT FILE: MOBAS

Some of the most popular competitive games are multiplayer online battle arenas, or MOBAs for short. These games came after a **mod** for an old strategy game called Warcraft 3: Reign of Chaos that originally landed in 2002. Modders adapted the real–time strategy game and gave it new rules, rules that are basically the same today. Players, controlling powerful hero characters, must battle each other, computer–controlled minions, and turrets located across three lanes, and work their way towards the enemy base to destroy the 'ancient' that resides there. The game mode was called Defense of the Ancients, or DOTA for short.

The first 'proper' game to be released in the MOBA style was League of Legends, or LoL for short (yes, most games in this *genre* have shortened names based on the initial letters of each word in their title – they're called acronyms). LoL follows the DOTA template quite closely, and as a result it is played by millions of people every day. It's also a free–to–play game, which means anyone can get stuck in if they want to, although non–paying players will have a limited number of characters to choose from. In fact, most MOBAs are free–to–play as it's hard to compete against huge titles like LoL if you're asking people to pay up front.

League of Legends is a hugely popular game, with professional teams competing in leagues around the world for cash prizes, but LoL can't compare to DOTA 2, another popular MOBA made by Valve (the company that runs the biggest PC gaming platform, Steam) that every year offers millions in prize money to the best teams. Those two games are monsters of the genre, but Blizzard rejoined the MOBA scene (after all, it was their game, Warcraft 3, that got this whole party started in the first place) with Heroes of the Storm. Bet you can't work out what that's called for short.

PRO TALK

Let's find out more about games by talking to some professionals. Gaming professionals are people who do something in gaming to earn a living, like making video games or writing about them in magazines. These pros really know their stuff – so let's hear their advice and tips.

JACK STEWART

Jack Stewart is an esports journalist – he writes about the latest gaming news and tournament results, and interviews professional players. Let's find out more…

1. WHY DO YOU THINK PEOPLE ENJOY ESPORTS?

"You want to win and prove you're the best. Watching the best players in the world is so fun and it's great getting to support your favourite team. I sit at home and cheer on my favourite League of Legends (LoL) and Overwatch teams the same way I cheer for my favourite football team."

2. WHAT WERE YOUR FAVOURITE GAMES AS A CHILD?

"I would play Pokémon non-stop for HOURS! Gold was the first one I played but Emerald will always be my favourite (Mudkip is my favourite starter). I also always picked up the new FIFA and WWE games every year; the Smackdown vs Raw series was especially great."

3. WHAT TIPS AND TRICKS CAN YOU GIVE US IF WE WANT TO GET BETTER AT GAMING?

"Other than practising, I'd say try to predict what your opponents are going to do. If you're one or two steps ahead of your enemies, you'll be able to surprise them and have the advantage. You also may not realise it but eating healthy food and exercising will help a lot too. You'll have more energy and your reaction times will be way faster; that's why you see a lot of esports players going to the gym!

4. WHAT ARE THE BEST AND WORST THINGS ABOUT YOUR JOB?

"The best part of my job is I get to travel around the world and write about the gaming tournaments that I love. The downside is I now don't have as much time to play games anymore, although I still manage to squeeze a few in!"

5. WHAT ADVICE WOULD YOU GIVE A YOUNG PERSON WHO WANTS TO GET INTO GAMING PROFESSIONALLY?

Find a game that you're good at and really enjoy playing, if you want to go pro you'll have to play that game for the next few years! If you're able to, watch replays of your own matches – seeing your gameplay from a different perspective will help you fix a lot of mistakes. Finally, I'd say once you get to a good level, make friends with pro players online. They'll give good advice and could help you join a team.

FACT FILE: OVERWATCH®

Blizzard don't do shooters, that's what people said. That was certainly the general opinion before Overwatch landed back in 2016. Nobody is saying that any more.

Overwatch has been growing steadily since its launch, with millions and millions of players signing up for duty in this online hero shooter over the past couple of years. The game launched with a range of colourful characters, but the secret to Overwatch's success is that the developers have never rested, with the game being regularly updated with new hero characters to learn, different maps to play on, and surprising game modes to keep things fresh.

Each Overwatch character is unique, and fulfils a special role on the battlefield. Mercy, for example, is what you would call a *support*, and although she won't do much damage to the enemy herself, her primary role is to heal her teammates and keep them in the fight. Hanzo, on the other hand, is a *damage dealer* and fires his deadly bow. Another damage specialist, Tracer, blinks through space, reappearing a few meters away from where she was last seen. *Tanks* like Winston are always on the frontline, absorbing damage while they keep the opponent busy. There are well over twenty heroes to choose from and each one has their own strengths and weaknesses.

As you play a typical game of Overwatch, players have to work together to achieve different objectives, such as protecting or attacking a certain section of the map. Teams have to coordinate, not just in the game, but in terms of the characters they choose to play as, and getting the right mix of characters is key to success.

As the *roster* of characters increases, so does the game's popularity. In 2018, Blizzard started OWL – the Overwatch League, and now professional teams and the best players around the world compete for glory.

CONTINUE?

Ok guys, it's time to take our places in the competition. With all this training, we can't lose! Let's go – or do you want a little more time before we head to the arena?

<<CONTINUE? Y/N>>
HTTPS://WWW.ESLGAMING.COM/

<<CONTINUE? Y/N>>
HTTPS://WWW.EASPORTS.COM/

<<CONTINUE? Y/N>>
HTTPS://WWW.SEAOFTHIEVES.COM/

<<CONTINUE? Y/N>>
HTTPS://PLAYOVERWATCH.COM/EN-GB/

<<CONTINUE? Y/N>>
HTTPS://WORLDOFWARCRAFT.COM/EN-GB/

GLOSSARY

4G — mobile communication that allows wireless internet access at very high speeds

battle royale — a fight involving many players that is fought until only one player remains

campaign — a continuing storyline or set of adventures

co-op — a type of game where two or more players can take part in the same storyline

damage dealer — players who are responsible for dealing out damage in the group

electronic — powered by electricity; usually a machine

engage — take part or become involved in

gearing up — improving your weapons or buying better ones

genre — a particular type or sort of something

inevitable — certain to happen

LAN — short for local area network, it refers to a group of computers that are physically connected to each other and let people play video games with each other without using the internet

loadout — a set of objects or weapons carried into battle

MOBAs — short for multiplayer online battle arenas, this is a type of game where the objective of the game is to overpower the opponents' team

mod — short for modification, a way to change a feature or format in a game

pixel — tiny dots of light that make up the images on a screen

roster — a list of the name of people in a group

shoulder buttons — also called bumpers, these are buttons on the edge of the controller above the trigger, often controlled with index fingers

simulations — replications of events or objects in real life

speciality — a skill or game someone is an expert at because they have practised it a lot

support — a type of character who is responsible for helping teammates with health or ammo

tanks — a character type that protects allies, disrupts enemies, and occupies the front line

unique — being the only one of its kind

<<SAVING KNOWLEDGE. DO NOT SHUT DOWN. SYSTEMS SHOW GOOD KNOWLEDGE RETENTION. WELL DONE.>>

INDEX